MOLISAN POEMS

SELECTED POEMS

D0899387

Essential Poets Series 83

Canadä

Guernica Editions acknowledge the financial support of the Government of Canada through the Book Publishing Industry Development Program (BPIDP).
This work was supported in part by a grant from the City University of New York PSC-CUNY Research Award program. This publication was assisted by the Minister of Foreign Affairs (Government of Italy) through the Istituto Italiano di Cultura in Toronto.

EUGENIO CIRESE

MOLISAN POEMS
SELECTED POEMS

TRANSLATED BY LUIGI BONAFFINI
AFTERWORD BY LUIGI BISCARDI
BILINGUAL EDITION

GUERNICA
TORONTO·BUFFALO·LANCASTER (U.K.)
2000

I dedicate this translation to the memory of Cosmo Marinelli.

Original Title: *Poesie Molisane* (1955)
Copyright © 2000, The Estate of Eugenio Cirese.
Translation © 2000, Luigi Bonaffini and Guernica Editions Inc.

Antonio D'Alfonso, editor.
Guernica Editions Inc.
P.O. Bo 117, Station P, Toronto (ON), Canada M5S 2S6
2250 Military Rd., Tonawanda, N.Y., 14150-6000 U.S.A.
Gazelle, Falcon House, Queen Square, Lancaster LA1 1RN U.K.

Typeset by Selina, Toronto.
Printed in Canada.

Legal Deposit — Third Quarter
National Library of Canada
Library of Congress Catalog Card Number: 99-64962
Canadian Cataloguing in Publication Data
Cirese, Eugenio, 1884-1955
Molisan poems : selected poems.
(Essential poets series ; 83)
Poems in Italian and English translation.
ISBN 1-55071-075-3
I. Bonaffini, Luigi. II. Title. III. Series.
PQ4809.I58M64   1999   851'.912   C99-900954-0

Contents

To Be a Child Again

New Poems

LIGHTNING

VARIOUS

Poesie Molisane

Al fratello Nicolino, morto nel 1950

Quacche lucecabella, Nicolì,
chi sa, pò esse ca tè luce e vule
capace a ravvivarte addò scié iute.
Puó quande vè l'estate
te porta nu salute
da dentr'all'uorte mieze a lu stellate.

Canzone d'atre tiempe

Duorme, bellezza mé', duorme serene
nu suonne luonghe quant'a la nuttata.

Molisan Poems

To My Younger Brother, Nicolino,
Who Died in 1950

Who knows, Nicolino, maybe a firefly
has sufficient light and wings
to bring a spark of life where you have gone.
Then, when summer comes,
they send you greetings
from the garden within the starlit sky.

Song of Long Ago

Sleep, my beauty, sleep serene
a sleep as long as the whole night.

Nen me lu dice

Suonne de paradise
fatte de cante
e d'allegria:
chi ze ce move dentre?
chi ntona la sunata
che te fa bella
e doce la iurnata
e la vocca te serra
a la parola?

Nen me lu dice,
nóne, ca i' nen c'entre:
sonna, nnucente, e porta
tu sola,
fin'a che campe 'n terra
ru suonne 'n core
e 'n mocca la risella.

Don't Tell Me

Dream of paradise
made of songs
and laughter:
who's stirring in it?
who plays the air
that makes your day
so beautiful and sweet
and seals your lips
to words?

Don't tell me,
because I'm not the one:
hold on to that dream, innocent girl,
and keep it in your heart,
a smile upon your lips,
you alone,
for as long as you are of this earth.

Serenatella

Iè notte e iè serene
dentr'a ru core e 'n ciele.
Le stelle
fermate
vicine,
a cócchia a cócchia
o sole,
com'a pecurelle
stanne pascenne
l'aria de notte
miez'a ru campe
senza rocchie
e senza fine.

Sponta la luna
e pare lu pastore
che guarda e conta
la mandra sparpagliata,
e z'assecura
che nisciuna
ze sperde
miez'a ru verde.
Canta nu rasciagnuole
la litania d'amore
dentr'a na fratta.

Serenade

It's nighttime
and heart and sky
are clear.
The stars
stopping
near,
in pairs
or alone,
graze
the night air
like sheep
in the field
without shrubs
and without end.

The moon comes out
and seems a shepherd
that watches and counts
the scattered flock,
and makes sure
that none
gets lost
amid the green.
A nightingale sings
a litany of love
inside a thicket.

Canta pe te
che viglie, bella,
e siente
la serenata
dent'a la stanza
areschiarata.

Nen t'addurmì, dulcezza,
veglia fin'a demane,
e penza a me che stonghe
a repenzà luntane,
e guarde
la luna ghiancha
che t'accarezza
e pare che t'arrenne
ridènne
ru vasce che te donghe.

It sings for you
who're still awake, my love,
and hear
the serenade
inside
the brightened room.

Don't fall asleep, my sweet,
stay awake till tomorrow,
and think of me lost
in my thoughts far away
while I watch
the white moon
its light touch
that seems to return
with a smile
the kiss I send you.

Via senza sole

Me ne so iute
a retruvà la via
ghianca de prète,
assulagnata,
guduta 'n cumpagnia,
te l'arecuorde?
Ma uoie senza sole,
scura, nfangata
l'éie aretruvata,
e sule ce camine
sperdute.

Scioscia ru viente
e pare nu lamiente
che dice:
l'amore nen ce sta.
Pe chesse
chiove ru ciele
e chiagne
la fratta senza sciure.
Tu pure
me sembre afflitte
ca nen te ride attuorne

Road Without Sun

I have gone
to find
the sundrenched road
paved with white stones
that we so enjoyed together,
do you remember?
But today
I found it
dark and muddy,
without sun,
and I am lost
walking on it alone.

The wind
seems a wail
that says
there is no love here.
That's why it rains
and the shrub weeps,
without flowers.
You too
seem sad
because the heart's sun
does not smile

ru sole de ru core
e quille
de ru ciele lucente,
che fa venì gulie
de vasce, de carezze
e de parole
sott'a na cèrca
tutta sfrunnata.
O sole, sole,
torna a schiarì ru ciele,
torna a fa ghianca
la via dell'amore.

and neither does the sun
in the luminous sky,
that makes you long
for a kiss, a touch,
for words
beneath a barren
oak tree.
O sun, sun,
come back to brighten the sky,
to whiten
the road of love.

Canzunetta

Tu vaie a la fonta
le panne a lavà,
l'amore t'affronta
t'aiuta a sciacquà.
La spara cumponne
la tina te pónne.

Tu vaie a ru bosche
la legna a fascià,
l'amore canosche
che vèn'a taglià.
La spara cumponne
ru fasce te pónne.

Tu vaie a la vigna
ca vuó velegnà,
l'amore la pigna
t'aiuta a taglià.
La spara cumponne
la cesta te pónne.

Tu vaie a ru liette
ca vuó repusà,
l'more a despiette
pe forza vò ntrà.
Ru liette accumponne
la treccia scumponne.

Tune

You go down to the spring
to wash all your clothes,
then love comes to bring
some help with the chores.
It fixes your headpad,
puts the jug on your head.

You go down to the forest
to bundle the firewood,
I know the love best
that severs for good.
It fixes your headpad,
puts the sheaf on your head.

You go to the vineyard
to do the grape harvest,
love gives you a hand
to cut down a cluster.
It fixes your headpad,
puts the basket on your head.

You go to your bed
to rest for the night
love out of spite
comes crashing ahead.
It fixes the bed
It loosens your braid.

Torna l'amore

Torna l'amore mie da la trincera,
iètte de vierne e vène a primavera.
Steva vestite a fridde ru Matese,
mo sta la ièrva fresca a le maiése.

Iè returnate tutt'all'ampruvvise,
senza durmì pe retruvà la sposa;
dentr'a la cambra sta lu paradise:
a vassa voce i' cante e z'arepose.

Ogne core

Ogne core scavata tè na buca,
cunchella de passione.
Ce càschene lucente
lacreme iuorne e notte,
antiche e sempre nove:
na nuvola dell'alma le fa chiove,
ru sole dell'amore, può, l'assuca.

Love Is Back

My love has just returned from the frontline,
he went in winter and came back in springtime.
The Matese was bundled white in snow,
and now there is fresh grass over the fallow.

He came back unexpected to his nest,
and weary from lost sleep to find his bride:
the little room holds paradise inside:
softly I sing and lull him to his rest.

Every Heart

Every heart has a niche
a small hollow of passion.
Night and day,
shining tears fall in,
ancient and always fresh:
they rain down from a cloud over the soul,
and then the sun of love dries them away.

Rosa sfrunnata

Chella rosa a ciente fronne
schiusa sola tra le spine
de na fratta de ciardine,
quacche vota tè la sorte
de n'amore desprezzate
scunsulate.

Tra le spine ze ntravede:
pare brutta e nze va ccoglie.
Ma se guarde può le foglie,
quande càschene ammusciate,
pass'aprile, magge passa
ma te lassa
dentr'a l'uocchie ru culore,
dentr'a l'anema l'addore.

Rose Without Leaves

The hundred-petaled rose
that grew alone among the thorns
of a bush inside the garden
now and then it meets the fortune
of a love that has been scorned
brokenhearted.

You can see it through the thorns:
it seem plain and you don't pick it.
But if then you watch the leaves,
when they fall to the ground wilted,
April passes, so does May
but on the way
in your eyes it leaves a brilliance
your soul's sweetened by its fragrance.

Suonne sperdute

Suonne d'amore mié, suonne d'amore,
pecché me scié lassate?
O suonne de passione, tradetore!
Dentr'a stu core stive arenzerrate
co na chiave d'argiente,
come 'n custodia l'ostie cunzacrate.
T'eva afferrate dope tanta stiente
pe mieze a nu padule,
na matina de sole, senza viente.
Ièva d'aprile: t'afferrave a vule,
co l'addore de rose;
d'allora éi' campate pe te sule.
E te sentiva pe tutte le cose
cantanne co na voce
che m'adduceva allegrezza e repose.

Mo, suonne bielle, appassiunate e doce
chiù de nu sucamèle,
me scié lassate com'a Criste 'n croce.
Suonne d'more mié sperdute 'n ciele,
com'a nu sciate d'ore,
suonne d'amore mié, suonne d'amore!

Lost Dream

My dream of love, o dream of love,
why have you left me?
O dream of passion ready to deceive!
You were locked with a silver key
within my heart, like a holy host
inside its case.
But after so much pain I found you at last
in a marshy place,
one sunny morning, with no sign of wind.
It was in April. I caught you in mid-air, among
the fragrant roses, and ever since I have lived
for you alone. In all things I heard your song
that left my soul in quiet calm and bliss.

Now, gentle dream, more passionate and sweet
than honeysuckle blossoms,
you've left me here like Christ upon the cross.
My dream of love lost in the sky,
my golden sigh,
o dream of love, my only dream of love!

Funtana secca

Funtana de repose
surgente de cunforto
nasciuta
miez'a le rose
e doppe tra le spine
scurruta
verse la fine
de chesta giuventù,
ru sole de settiembre
t'à retruvata
seccata.

Ghianche tra la verdura
a tuorn'a tuorne
a la surgiva
tanne ridévene
le margarite
e me dicevene
sempre ca scì,
quande ch'i' le sfrunnava.
Le fronne reguardava
purtate lente lente
da la currente
luntane,

Dry Fountain

Fountain of peace
spring of comfort
born
among the roses
you flowed among thorns
toward the end
of youth,
and the September sun
found you
bone dry.

White amid the green
the daisies
round
the wellspring
were all smiles then,
and when I plucked them
always said yes to me.
I watched the leaves
carried slowly
by the current
far away,

e l'uocchie m'abbagnava
quande l'amore
me faceva suffrì.

E mo?
Dentr'a ru fuosse sicche
càschene fronne gialle.
Le margarite ze sò ppassite,
e sule, a balle,
miez'a ru spine
che segna ru cunfine
de chesta giuventù,
nat'è nu sciore
senz'acqua e senz'addore.

Sciurille de passione,
de lacrime vurrìa
nnacquarte,
ma l'uocchie tienghe assutte
a lu suffrì;
la funtanella è secca,
scioscia la vòria
e me canta la storia
de l'amore distrutte.
Te guarda senza chiante
murì,
sciore de campusante.

and my eyes moist
when love
made me suffer.

And now?
Yellow leaves fall
into the dry basin.
The daisies
have withered,
and downstream, solitary
among the thorns
that mark the boundary
of this youth,
a flower was born
without water or scent.

Little passion flower,
I'd like to sprinkle you
with tears, but my eyes
have grown dry
to sorrow;
the small fountain has no water,
the north wind starts to blow
and sings me a tale
of shattered love.
I watch you die
without a tear,
cemetery bloom.

L'acqua e l'amore

L'amore iè come na currenta d'acqua
ch'è chiara a la surgiva,
e dentre ze ce specchia e ze ce sciacqua
la ierva de la riva.
La ierva de la riva z'addecreia
e l'acqua l'accarezza e murmureia.

Passa, repassa, vota, z'areggira
sott'a nu pontecielle;
parla chiù forte a notte quande mira
la luna e ciente stelle.
La luna e ciente stelle 'n funne serra:
ze crede che sta 'n ciele, ma sta 'n terra.

La china la straporta a la chianura
chiù lèggia e senza funne.
Spuma, sgrezzeia e senz'avé paura
ntravede ru sprufunne.
Ntravede ru sprufunne e pure scorre,
e quand'è chiù vicine chiù ce corre.

Quand'è rrivata a balle e vò repose,
nu liette iè de lota.
Le racanelle càntene annascose;
da monte vè l'accòta.
Da monte vè l'accota ntruvedata
e l'acqua vòlle e sbatte sdellezzata.

Allaca le campagne, le turmenta,
va rregne quacche buca.
E quande nn'aretrova la currenta
la terra ze la suca.
La terra ze la suca chiane chiane;
dó steva l'acqua resta nu pantane.

Water and Love

Love is like the water of a flowing stream
clear at the fountainhead
the grass upon the bank peeks in its gleam
and splashes in its bed.
The grass upon the bank is having fun,
the water strokes it and it murmurs on.

It passes back and forth, it turns, it loops
under the narrow bridgespan;
at night its voice gets louder when it looks
up at the hundred stars around the moon.
It locks the moon and stars within its depths:
It thinks it's in the sky, but it's on earth.

The slope returns it to the plain below
lighter and bottomless.
It foams, it splatters, and with no fear at all
it stares into the abyss.
It stares into the abyss and yet it flows,
as it gets nearer, the faster on it goes.

When it hits bottom and it tries to rest,
it finds a bed of mud.
The hidden tree-toads sing from their green nest;
from upstream comes the flood.
The flood comes from upstream darkened and cloudy.
the water boils and churns in spinning eddies.

It overflows the countryside, torments it,
it fills the holes around.
And when it can no longer find the current
it seeps into the ground.
It seeps into the ground little by little;
where there was water now there's only a wallow.

33

Canzone d'atre tiempe

I' parte pe na terra assai luntana,
l'amore m'accumpagna e me fa lume.
A notte passe e beve a la funtana,
me ferme a la pagliara 'n faccia a sciume.
Ma l'acqua de la fonte è n'acqua amara,
repose chiù nen trove a la pagliara.

Nen tenghe chiù pariente né cumpagne,
nen tenghe chiù na casa pe reciétte;
perciò mo vaglie spiérte, e nen me lagne,
ca tu me rieste, amore benedette!
Te sola m'à lassata ru destine,
lampa che scalle e nzegne ru camine.

La via è longa e sacce addò me porta:
me porta a nu castielle affatturate
dó campene la gente senza sorta,
dó scorde ru dolore appena ntrate.
Tu famme core a core cumpagnia,
nen fa stutà la lampa pe la via.

Song of Times Past

I'm leaving for new shores and faroff mountains
accompanied by love that lights my way.
At night I pass and drink down at the fountain.
I stop at the river by the mound of hay.
But now the water has a bitter taste,
the hayrick can no longer give me rest.

I have no longer a relative or friend,
I do not have a house or roof above;
and so I wander lost, but do not bend,
because I still have you, my blessed love!
You alone my fate didn't take away
lamp that gives me warmth and shows the way.

The road is long, and I know where it takes:
it takes me to an old enchanted fortress
where only ill-starred people put up stakes,
where once inside I'll soon forget my sadness.
Stay closer to my heart, be company,
don't ever let the light die out for me.

La fatìa

Lu pecurare

Le pecure ammucchiate e a coccia sotte
pàscene ierva e dicene: va bè;
ru cane corre e abbaia iuorne e notte.
Lu pecurare
va nnanze e rrète a recuntà la mandra
e spisse spisse
ze ietta 'n terra a la supina.

Veiàte a isse:
pecure a recuntà,
ciele a vedé e terra a caminà.

Work

The Shepherd

The sheep in a big heap, head to the ground,
graze on the grass and say: this is all right;
the dog bolts here and there, barks day and night.
The shepherd
saunters to and fro to count the flock,
and now and then he stretches on his back,
on the bare earth.

And he is a lucky boy:
the sheep to count,
a ground to walk on, and a sky to enjoy.

Camina

Da 'n coppa all'uorte
sembrava na furmica
pe ru tratture.
Annanze e arrète
matina e sera:
a scegne la matina,
a renchianà la sera
sudate e stanche,
la zappa 'n cuolle
e pède nnanze pède, tranche tranche.

— Zì Minche, è calle.
— Frische è ru sciume.
— Zì Minche, è fridde.
— Zappe e me scalle.
D'estate e dentr'a vierne,
sempre la stessa via,
isse, la zappa e la fatìa.

Walk

From the garden rail
he looked like an ant
down there on the sheep trail.
Back and forth
morning and evening:
down in the morning,
back up at sunset,
dust and sweat,
the hoe on his shoulder
step by step, slow as a snail.

"Zì Minche, it's hot."
"The river is cool."
" Zì Minche, it's cold."
"I'll keep warm hoeing."
Summer's ending, winter's behind,
the same road always,
him, the hoe, the daily grind.

1949

Na vota l'anne
'n coppa a le spalle
nu sacchitte de grane:
lu tuozze de pane.
La zappa pe magnà,
lu pane pe zappà.

Puó na bella matina
zì Minche sbagliatte la via,
pigliatte chella de Santa Lucia
purtate a quattre.

Repose

Forse che l'ome z'è ssupite
dope la fateiàta de ru iuorne,
lassa 'n terra lu cuorpe appesantite
e ze va a mette 'n ciele
pe gode lu repose
a lume de le stelle.
Ru ventarielle
pare che t'areporte lu respire
e lu Befiérne
arrima le parole
e fa sentì lu cante de lu suonne.

Nu rasciagnuole,
da chi sa dó, responne.

1949

1949

Once a year
a little sack of wheat
upon his shoulders.
His piece of bread.
The hoe to be able to eat,
the bread to be able to hoe.

Then one morning
zì Minche took the wrong turn,
he was carried to Santa Lucia
never to return.

Rest

Maybe as soon as man starts to doze off
after a day of long backbreaking work,
he leaves his oppressed body down on earth
and climbs across the sky
to enjoy his rest
by the light of the stars.
The gentle breeze now seems
to bring you back your breath
and the Biferno
makes every word a rhyme
and lets you listen to the song of dreams.

From somewhere far
a nightingale replies after a time.

1949

La fatìa

Tutte a munne ne vè pe la fatìa,
vòria de vierne e grànera d'estate;
chi la recerca e chi la maledice,
chi ne tè troppa e chi la vularrìa.
E iè pesante sule a numenarla,
ma quande chiù te pesa
chiù te la puorte 'n cuolle.
Chi sa dice nu "libbera nosdòmene"
pe lassarne li figlie alleggerite?

Déteme lla lanterna de magàre
ca vuoglie addeventà nu metetore
e mète la fatìa
p'ogne campe de munne
da cape a piede l'anne, senza suonne.
Trascenarmela può co nu strascine,
arrammucchiarla tutta 'n copp'a n'ara
e purtarmela appriesse quande i' more.

1948

Hard Work

The whole world can't see straight because of work,
north wind in winter and in summer hail;
and there are those who seek it, those who curse it,
those who have too much and those who want it.
And it feels heavy just to talk about it,
and yet the more it weighs you down
the more you carry it on your back.
Who can say a *libbera nosdòmene*
to leave his children with a lighter weight?

Give me the lantern of the sorcerer
because I want to be a harvester
and harvest hard work
in every field in the world
all year long, without sleep or rest.
Then tow it on a handcart out the door
and pile it up out on the threshing floor
to take it with me on the day I die.

1948

Spera de sole

Ciele ncupite,
furia de viente e neve a sciucculille.
Cilì de passarielle nfreddolite,
uauà de guagliuncielle mananute.

E Tu scié remenute
a suone de sampogna
e de campane a festa,
pe repurtà speranza a lu suffrì.

Spera de sole mieze a la tempesta.

O gente, gente!

Ummìsce.

O gente, gente!
Renzerrate le pècure,
arentrate le cunnule,
rencruciate le fàvece,
scampaneiate a grànera.

Ray of Sunlight

Darkening skies,
fury of wind, flurries of snow-crystals.
Tweet-tweet of shivering sparrows,
naked children's cries.

And you have come back
with the sound of bagpipes
and joyful bells,
to bring a gleam of hope to those who suffer.

Ray of sunlight across the raging storm.

O People, People!

It's thundering in the distance.

O people, people!
Lock in the sheep.
Bring in the cradle.
Cross over the scythes,
ring the bells in the hailstorm.

Resta qua 'n terra

Pecchè la pace te la puorte 'n ciele?
Dope la passione
Criste Gesù risorte
falla na Pasqua senza l'ascenzione.

P'avé la pace te mettierne 'n croce
ma p'avé pace nen facieste guerra.

Aiutece a rescì da stu sprufunne,
fa resentì la voce de lu galle
a chi te l'à fermate e le rinchioda
le vraccia aperte p'abbraccià lu munne.

'N eterne

Ogge, lu pane.
Iere, lu recurdà.
Ogge, iere, demane.

Lu vinnele trapàna la matassa,
z'aggliommera lu file e scorre e passa.

Pàssene le iurnate longhe e corte,
pàssene a un'a una estate e vierne.
Iè nu succede che nen sembra vere
sta vita che camina
a rabbraccià la morte.
Ogge e demane: jere.
'N eterne.

Stay Here on Earth

Why do you always take peace back to heaven?
After the passion
Christ Jesus risen
let one Easter pass without the Ascension.

To have their peace they put you upon the cross
but to have peace you did not wage them war.

Help us out of the abyss where we've been hurled,
let the voice of the cock be heard once more
by those who once held down, and now are nailing,
your arms thrown open to embrace the world.

For Ever

Today, bread.
Yesterday, remembering.
Tomorrow, starting over.
Today, yesterday, tomorrow.

The winder unravels the long skein,
the thread begins to wind, it runs and spins.

Days long and short go by, one by one
summers and winters go by.
This life that walks
into the arms of death.
doesn't seem real.
Today and tomorrow, yesterday.
For ever.

LUCECABELLE

Pover'amore

Ru munne è viecche e ce ne sò passate
speranze a fa sunnà la cuntentezza.
Lu tiempe de gudè nn'è mai venute,
e tu, pover'Amore scanusciute,
te sciè nnascuse sotte a le Tre croce
a chiagne senza voce.

La pecura

Da quande lu Pastore
ze la mettètte 'ncuolle,
mentre pasce lu Bene va cercanne.
Lu Bene va chiamanne
quande l'ome la porta a ru macièlle.
E mentre grama e z'alluntana,
lassa a le spine nu sciocche de lana.
Lu liette pe le reninelle.

1949

Fireflies

Poor Love

The world is old, so many hopes have passed
to make us dream of happiness.
The time for pleasure never came
and you, poor Love without a name,
hid under the Three Crosses
to shed your tears alone and voiceless.

The Sheep

From the time the Shepherd
put her on his shoulders,
she keeps on looking for the Good while grazing.
She keeps on calling for the Good
when man takes her to slaughter.
And as she's led away and moans,
she leaves a flock of wool
caught in the thorns,
a bed for swallows.

1949

Sule

A balle lu sciume lucente
ze stenne a la luna e me manna
na voce accurata.
Che vò?

Nze smove na prèta, nze sente
nu sfrusce; lu core z'affanna
sul'isse e camina.
Dó va?

Nu cane mo bbaia a la luna.
Dó sta?

1949

Alone

Downstream the shimmering river
extends in the moonlight and sends me
his anguished voice.
What can he want?

No stone is moving, you don't hear a shiver;
the heart alone
goes anxiously on.
Where is it going?

And now a dog is howling at the moon.
From where?

E mo?

Chell'atra vota
— dó fu e quande? —
chi sa s'è state vere o fu nu suonne.
Nu ciele abbrevedite
e nire come a la paura.
E fridde e puzza e lóta,
e sanghe e fame e arzura
e trìtteche de morte.
Ma la notte na voce de cunfuorte
luntana te veniva.
La casa
dó nu fuoche scallava,
na cannéla schiariva,
na crona perdunava.

E mo?
La morte 'n piette e le macère attuorne.
Nu chiante de sampogna.
E la lemosena de chi t'à ccise
stenne le vracce
e te sceppa lu core. La vergogna
à perduta la faccia.

1949

And Now?

That other time
— where was it and when? —
who knows if it was real or was a dream.
A shivering sky
black as fear.
And cold and stench and mud,
and hunger and thirst and blood
and shuddering of death.
But from far off
a voice of peace returned
during the night.
The house
where a fire burned,
a candle gave light,
a rosary forgave.

And now?
Death inside and ruins all around.
A bagpipe's wailing sound.
And the charity of those who have slain you
extends its arms in an embrace
and tears at your heart. Shame
has lost its face.

1949

Ritorne

Me guàrdene le case a uocchie apierte:
— Quisse chi iè?
Da donda vè? —
La casa méia
tè l'uocchie chiuse e morta pare.

Sciume, tu sule tié la stessa voce,
tu sule, sciume, m'é recanusciute.
Chi songhe, donda venghe
e dó so iute spierte,
raccóntele a lu mare.

1945

Niente

Né fuoche né liette né pane
né sciate de vocca
né rima de cante
né calle de core.
Niente.
— E tu? e tu? e quille?
Niente.
Finitoria de munne.
L'uocchie sbauttite
iè ssutte.

1945

Return

The houses look at me
with open eyes that ask, "Who is he?
Where does he come from?"
My house
keeps its eyes shut and it appears dead.

River, only you have the same voice,
only you, river, recognize me.
Who I am, where I come from
and where I wandered lost,
go tell it to the sea.

1945

Nothing

Neither fire nor bed nor bread
nor breath from a mouth
nor rhyme from a song
nor the warmth of a heart.
Nothing.
"And you? and you? and him?"
Nothing.
The world is in ruins.
The eyes, bewildered,
are dry.

1945

Ecche la Stella

La meza luna stanca ze ne cala
arrete a lu Matese.

Ecche a la Stella,
ecche a Maria
la picculella,
ecche a ru Lupe ncatenate.
Le Gallenelle stanne ammasciunate
e la Speranza
lùceca appena pe la luntananza.

Una, du, tre e quattre.
Patre Figlie e Spirite Sante.
Chella è la Croce
che ze l'abbraccia a tutte quante.

There Is the Star

The weary half-moon sets
behind the Matese mountains.

There is the Star,
there is Mary
the little one,
there is the Wolf in chains.
The Hens are gathered in their coop
and Hope
is a faint glimmer from afar.

One, two, three and four,
Father, Son and Holy Ghost.
There is the Cross
embracing one and all.

Repuote

Com'era doce lla parola
quande me la decìve: iessa sola
bastava a farme areturnà guaglione:
— Figlie mié, figlie. —
Scié morta, mamma,
nen songhe chiù figlie.

Dentre a lu core sente nu resuone:
— Se la vocca vò ride
o l'uocchie z'è ppannate,
ca lu core fa male,
recanta na canzone
de lu tiempe passate.
    — Dì, quale, mamma, quale?

— Lùceca lùceca, lucecabella . . . —
Tutta la terra relucecheiava
e me sembrava pur'essa nu ciele.
Mamma, te ne scié iuta tu
e nen lùceca niente chiù.

Guardave dentr'a l'uocchie e me capive
e na parola tèia m'abbastava.
Decìve:
— Alza l'uocchie 'n ciele:
la negghia ze ne va da lu cervielle
dó rèstene le stelle. —
Come tu le decìve sse parole
nesciune le sa dice.
Tutte ru ciele
ze ne calava dentr'a ru ciardine.

Death Song

The word was a sweet sound
when said by you: it was enough
to make me a child again:
"Son, my son."
You have died, mother,
I'm no longer a son.

In my heart there's a lingering echo:
"If your lips want to smile
or your eyes have been dimmed
by the pain in your heart,
sing a song for a while
from a time long ago.
Tell me which one, mother, which?

"Fire, fire, firefly . . ."
The whole earth was on fire
and it too seemed a sky.
Mother, you have passed away
and nothing shines today.

You looked into my eyes and understood me,
a word from you was all I needed.
You said:
"Raise your eyes to the sky:
the mist will leave your brain
and only stars remain. "
No one can ever say
those words like you.
The whole sky
descended in the garden.

Chi me dà chiù cunforte e chiù cunsiglie?
Scié morta, mamma.
Nen songhe chiu figlie.

Ottant'anne so tante a fa la conta
e tante pe suffrirle;
ma quande z'arraconta
e sò passate,
iè come fusse state nu salustre;
na lampa e puó lu scure.
Lu decìve tu pure:
— Eh, la vita che iè?
Ciuciù ciuciù ciuciù,
vuvù vuvù.

E puó?
Na iapèrta de vocca e iè finite.
La ntima pe campà mo dó la piglie?
Iè finite, mamma. Nen songhe chiù figlie.

1949

Now who will give me comfort and advice?
Mother, you have died.
I'm no longer a son.

Eighty years are so many when you count them
and so many to have to suffer through;
but when you tell it
and they're gone,
it seems as if they'd been a flash of light;
a flicker and then darkness.
You said so too:
"Eh, what is life?"

And then?
Your lips unclose and it's all over.
Where do I find the courage to go on?
It's over, mother,
I'm no longer a son.

1949

Lucecabella

La cuntentezza
de la nnucenza,
de lu ricorde
la lucentezza.
De la festa chiù bella dell'ome
l'alluminazione.

Lucecabella,
nasciuta da na lacrema de mèle,
na stella te facette da cummara,
e te mettette n'angele ru nome.
Tu me fai crede che lu munne è buone,
i' pe te sacce come ze sta n' ciele.

Respire

Respire de prima matina
acquara de lu core:
m'allegerisce
com'a na calandrella
e vóle senza scénne.

Firefly

The happiness
of innocence,
memory's
brightness.
Illumination
for man's most beautiful feast.

Firefly,
born from a tear of honey,
your godmother was a star,
an angel gave you your name.
You can make me believe the world is good,
through you I know what heaven would be like.

Breath

Early morning breath
heart's dew:
it makes me as light
as a skylark
and I fly without wings.

Vulà

Tutte le ciélle vólene;
ce sta quille che sfarfalleía
tra pénce e rama;
e ce sta quille che sa rrivà
mieze a ru ciele
co na scennata.

L'astore

Vulà come a n'astore
che fa la rota attuorne a le muntagne,
vénce lu viente e segna ru cunfine
da cima a cima.

Damme la mane

Appiccia la cannéla e famme luce
ca vuoglie arecercà chi ze n'è iute,
ca vuoglie aretruvà chi z'è sperdute
miez'a lu scure.

Damme la mane e iesce a lu scupierte.
La terra ancora fuma,
lu sole ancora scalla,
e la ventima nàzzeca le spiche.

1949

To Fly

All birds fly;
there is the one that flits
from branch to rooftile;
and then there is the one
that reaches the sky
with one stroke of its wings.

The Hawk

To fly like a goshawk
that circles the mountains,
conquers the wind and marks the boundary
from summit to summit.

Give Me Your Hand

Light the candle and shine it on the road.
I want to search for those who have gone away,
I want to go find those who've gone astray
in the deep darkness.

Give me your hand and come out in the open.
The earth is still smoking, the sun
is still warm,
and the wind slowly rocks the ears of corn.

1949

Returnà guaglione

Vierne

Svegliarme a mezanotte,
aresentì ru sciusce de la vòria
che vè da Petravalle,
e dell'arlogge de ru campanile
lu suone de cuccégne.

D'arrète a la finestra
accumpagnà co l'uocchie mentre scegne
nu cencione de neve.

Scappà senza cappotte
p'ammantarme de fridde
e remané sperdute
mieze a lu sciuccature.

Sunnà

Nutà pell'aria com'a dentr'all'acqua,
arrafferrà na corna de la luna,
llungà na mane p'acchiappà na stella.
Nu itteche e nu zumpe 'n 'copp'a liette,
e puó n'abballuttata pe ru ciele.

1950

To Be a Child Again

Winter

To wake up at midnight,
to hear the north wind's breath
coming from Pietravalle,
and the earthen clunk
of the bellfry clock.

From behind the window
to follow a falling snowflake
with my eyes.

To run coatless
wrapped in cold
and stand lost
amid the snowfall.

Dream

To swim across the air as if in water,
to reach and grasp the sharp horn of the moon,
to extend my hand until I catch a star.
A sudden start, a leap over the bed,
and then to fall and tumble through the sky.

1950

E niente chiù

Pigliarla a vule na lucecabella,
stritarla com'allora 'n front'a te.
Aresentì la voce che chiamava:
— Ugè, Ugè. —

'N coppa a lu monte

Arenchianà lu monte sule sule,
dell'aria attuorne iesse chiù leggiere,
vedé lu sciume
come nen fusse vere,
nen sentirme chiù 'n terra
e pussède lu munne.

Pasqua

Iaprì la porta de ru campanare,
nchianà pe chella scala com'a grille.
Fferrà la funa de ru campanone
e risentì la Pasqua
co l'onna de llu suone.

And Nothing Else

To catch a firefly in flight,
to crush it just like then before your eyes.
To hear once more the voice that used to call me:
"Ugè, Ugè."

On the Mountain

To climb the mountain all alone,
to be as light as the surrounding air,
to see the river
as if it were unreal,
to feel myself no longer of this earth
and own the world.

Easter

To open wide the door of the bellfry
and scamper up that ladder like a cricket.
To grasp the rope of the enormous bell
and listen to Easter
on the wave of the knell.

Ninnanonna

Putesse arresentì da 'n coppa'all'ara
de chella ninnanonna lu resuone:
— Duorme bellezza mé, duorme serene
nu suonne luonghe quant'a la nuttata.—

Pe cùnnula n'acchione,
attuorne attuorne
festa de grille e de lucecabelle
e come a na cuperta trapuntata
nu ciele tutte stelle.

L'utema nchianata

A lume de na luce appennetora
putesse arrevederla chella mane
che segnava pe l'aria
la via de ru cunte longa longa
de le sette muntagne.
Putesse com'allora
aresentì la voce
a dirme chiane chiane:
— Fatte curagge:
la sèttima muntagna è avvicinata.
Allàccete le scarpe
pe l'ùtema nchianata.—

70

Lullaby

If I could only hear, out on the threshing floor,
the echo of that lullaby once more:
"Sleep, my little darling, and sleep tight
a sleep that lasts as long as the whole night."

A sheaf for a cradle,
and everywhere around
a revelry of fireflies and crickets
and like an embroidered blanket
a star-blazoned sky.

The Last Climb

If only I could see that hand
move by the light of a hanging lantern
and trace in the air again
the long, long road from the tale
of the seven mountains.
If I could hear
that voice softly say:
"Be brave: the seventh mountain's near
The time has come
to tie your shoes
for the last climb."

Nuove poesie

Guaglione

Addò te truove,
addò te muove,
tutte è na guagliunèra.

Tu gire a tunne,
ma iè ru munne
che pazzéia co te.

N'atre guaglione
sta a fa lu giratunne
pe lu passate,
ca dentre a lu demane spedalate
iè tutte zitte.

Nunziatina

Nu libbre apierte nnanze e può richiuse,
e l'uocchie llà dall'uorte.
Cantava Nunziatina e ru telare
ièva l'accorde.

Nu cante e na guardata;
nu libbre apierte e chiuse.
Nunziatina, tu
pazzìa
de chella giuventù,
frescura
de lu recuorde.

NEW POEMS

Child

Whatever you do,
wherever you go,
everything's child's play.

You go around in a whirl,
but then it's the world
that capers with you.

Another child
does ring-around-a-rosy
through the past,
for in tomorrow's wasteland
all is silence.

Nunziatina

A book open before her and then closed,
her gaze beyond the garden.
Nunziatina sang and the loom
was her accompaniment.

A song and her gaze;
a book opened and closed.
Nunziatina, you
folly
of that youth,
freshness
of memory.

Lu pulletrielle

A Michele Pierri

Lassa la menna.
Stizze de latte caschene;
Bianchina la cavalla capezzéia.

— Tè, pulle pulle pulle. —
Mo trotta a la chiamata:
la lénga raspa 'n faccia;
la ièrva addora
E nen sa ancora
ca lu sciore ze magna.

Ze iétteca:
lampe de fuoche pàssene pe l'uocchie.
Sule isse sente lu rechiame
e corre corre corre.

Nuvole 'n ciele, passene le mandre.

Ze nfroscia e casca
— quattre bastune ze sò fatte zampe —
e vatte l'aria e ze remette allérta
e guarde arrète.

Nu strille:
l'ha vista e mo ze la remira
la mamma tutta ghianca
mieze a lu rusce de la lupinella.

The Colt

To Michele Pierri

He leaves the teat.
Drops of milk trickle;
Bianchina the mare nods her head.

"Here, here, come on."
Now he trots to the call,
tongue rasping against cheek;
the grass has a strong smell
and he still doesn't know
flowers are good to eat.

He has a start:
flashes of fire flicker through his eyes.
He alone hears the cry
and runs runs runs.

The herds are passing through, clouds in the sky.

He huffs and falls
— four sticks have become legs —
he flails the air and gets back on his feet
and looks behind him.

A shriek:
he has seen her and now he looks
toward his mother, all white
in the red of the sainfoin.

Prucessione

Annanze annanze, loche a balle
— ze vede e nen ze vede —
na cosa ghianca:
nu guagliuncielle.

Na palluccella de vammascia
che ze trascina appriesse
la prucessione.

Gnora zia

La capellèra tutte le matine.
Nu tuppe 'n cape
com'a na calandrella
e cricca cricca.
Na mane stesa
pe fàrsela vascià.

Mieze a du déte
nu cannelline.

Zì Micalangele

Zì Micalangele senza zimarra,
la vavarola nera e ru cullare,
a parlà sule
dentre a na cambra chiuse
isse e nu Garibalde aretrattate.

Procession

Down there, way up in front
— you can barely see it —
something white:
a little boy.

A tiny ball of cotton
with the procession
in tow.

Dear Aunt

The hairdresser every morning.
A lark-like bun
atop her head,
and sitting upright.
A hand extended
to be kissed.

A sugared almond
pressed between two fingers.

Zì Michelangelo

Zì Michelangelo without his long coat,
black mantelet and collar,
talking to himself
inside a closed room.
Him and a painted Garibaldi.

Zì Salvie

Zì Salvie: dope tant'anne, sempe
ogne matina,
annanze a llu purtone t'arrassiette
a fa designe all'aria
co lu bastone,
a mette
na risatella
pe denttr'all'ora afflitta de llu tiempe.

Sole de vierne

Nu sulecielle
che ze n'è sciute apposta da la negghia
pe fa rrivà na spera e dà nu fiate
a llu curnicchie de purtone
addó alméia,
de sotte
nu cence de cappotte,
nu mucchietiélle d'ossa arrannecchiate.

La miendra

Ru ballecone sempre spalancate;
nnanze la miendra:
la mendrélla de sotte all'uorte,
de primavera
tutta nu sciore.
Puó na ielata,
e a la stagione
sole tre miéndre aperte 'n cima 'n cima

Zì Salvie

Zì Salvio: after so many years,
always, every morning,
you sit before the doorway
and with your cane
make scrawls in the air
to lay
a chuckle
upon the melancholy hour of our time.

Winter Sun

A faint sun
that has come out on purpose from the fog
to send a shaft of light and give some breath
to the niche in the doorway
where a huddled pile of bones
wheezes softly
beneath a ragged coat.

The Almond Tree

The balcony is open wide as always,
across from it the almond tree.
The little almond tree in the kitchen garden,
all in bloom
in the springtime.
Then a frost,
and in the summer
only three almonds unclosing way on top.

Ballecone

Sàmmel'a dice, cielle volavola:
chi l'ha guardate tutte lu biancore,
chi ze l'è sentute
tutte lu bell'addore
de tanta primavere rose schiuse?
Chianta de rose ghianche
remasta sola sola
'n copp'a ru ballecone.

Che bella luna

Na madunnella messa 'n ballecone.
Chi sa se lu recuorde
z'aggira a donde sta:
tre ore sule sule
dentre a la stanza,
senza nu vasce.

Che bella luna 'n ciele a faccia chiena!

Spazeià

A Ferruccio Ulivi

Ancora te ce affacce a la vetrata
addó stev'addurmite llu sperdute
che te vuleva bene
e nzieme a te venive mananute
a spazeià pe mieze a lu serene,
luna che a tiempe a tiempe nchiane 'n ciele.

Balcony

Can you tell me, bird on the wing,
who looked at all that whiteness,
who smelled
that heady scent
of so many spring roses unfolding?
White rosebush
left all alone
out on the balcony.

What Lovely Moon

A small madonna placed out on the balcony.
Who knows if memory
is turning where she is:
three hours all alone
inside a room,
without a kiss.

What a lovely full-faced moon up in the sky.

Range

Do you still stop to peek through the same window
where, fast asleep, you looked at the lost soul
who really loved you
and would go wandering naked by your side
to range amid the night without a cloud
moon that slowly rise across the sky.

Lu muortecielle

I

Te porta la ventima e z'areporta
lu suone a gloria de na campanella.
le prime stizze
z'allàrghene pe terra.
Nu guaglione tè 'n mane ru tragnitte
e zómpa pe le prète;
na mamma porta 'n cape
ru tavutielle
e corre ppriesse all'acceprete.
Cuscì lu citulille
ze ne va scappa scappa
pure a ru campusante.

II

Lu porta 'n cape a lu repose,
la mamma sé,
come ze lu purtava
'n campagna e puó lu nazzecava
cantanne all'ombra de la cèrca.
— O sonni sonni,
vien'a a cavalle a nu cavalle bianche.—
Mo lu sonni
tutt'all'ampruvvise
a notte scura iè rrivate
a cavalle a nu cavalle nire,
e a lu citrille
pe sempre ha chiuse l'uocchie
senza la ninna nonna.
Nen tè piedi la cùnnula
che mamma mentre chiove porta 'n cape:
lu figlie che ze c'è addurmite
nn'ha chiù bisogne d'èsse nazzecate.

82

The Dead Child

I

The light wind brings the mournful toll
of distant bells, and carries back its echo.
The first drops
spread upon the ground.
A little boy holds the aspergillum in his hand
and skips over the pavingstones;
a mother carts a small coffin
on her head
and hurries after the priest.
So the child slips away
running
even to his grave.

II

She carries him to his rest upon her head,
his mom,
the way she used to carry him
to the fields, and cradle him
singing beneath the shade of the old oak.
"O sleep, sleep,
come riding a white horse."
But sleep
suddenly
has come
riding a black horse,
and the child
has closed his eyes forever
without a lullaby.
The cradle that mom carries on her head
under the rain, doesn't have legs:
the son who fell asleep
Doesn't need to be rocked any more.

III

Chiù de la notte
la casa z'è scurita.
Vè da sotte terra
llu chiante.

Chiante de mamma.
Chiante de ciele e munne.
Pe nu citrille.
Nen vo lu pane,
nen vo repose
la mamma sé: vò chiagne.

Vò rregne lu core assutte
pe chiagne.
La mamma sé.

IV

La palla
pare che corre ancora
sotte a la seggiulella.
Quande ha finite a chiagne
la mamma sé,
la va a reponne
dentr'a la cascia,
e quand'è morta
ce la reporta,
pe vederle iucà
tutta la ternità.

III

The house has darkened
deeper than the night.
The weeping comes
from underneath the ground.

A mother's weeping,
weeping of sky and world.
For a small child.

She doesn't want bread,
she doesn't want rest,
his mom: she wants to cry.

She wants to fill her barren heart
to cry.
His mom.

IV

The ball
seems to be bouncing still
under the little chair.
When she has stopped her crying
his mom
puts it inside the chest,
and when she dies
will bring it to him,
to watch him play
through all eternity.

Llu muortecielle, che sorte.
Nen sapé che la morte
iè cosa accuscì grossa.
Nen cresce,
nen vedé lache de luna,
né code de cumète
né eclisse de sole
a scurrèie la terra;
nen sentì tuone nè afa de calle
nè pese de zappa;
ìrsene a lu ripose scappa scappa,
purtate 'ncape da mamma
a suone de campana a gloria.
Lassà na palla pe memoria
che mamma t'areponne
e puó te la reporta
quande z'è morta.
Avé de mamma
lu chiante d'afflizione,
dentr'a nu core de mamma
remané guaglione.

V

A dead child's fate.
Not to know that death
is something so very big.
Not to grow up,
not to see moon lakes,
nor comet tails
nor eclipses of the sun
to darken earth;
not to hear thunder nor feel heat
or weight of hoe;
to slip away racing to his rest, to go
carried on his mom's head
through mournful tolls.
To leave behind the memory of a ball
that your mom puts away
and then brings back to you
the day she dies.
To hear your mother's
weeping of affliction,
within a mother's heart
remain a child.

All'aria fina

All'aria fina
de lla muntagna méia,
i' sule sule,
a resentirme dentre
lu vàttete de core,
e fore
a refiatà la vita
co lu suspire de la matutina.

1953

Nuvuletta

Fume de bomma de na festa 'n ciele.
'N faccia a lu sole
com'a nu vele
ze stènne, z'atturcina;
ze vede appena appena
e ze nserena.

A la matina 'n terra arecumpare
na negghiarella mbossa
ch'arracumponne
'n copp'a le fronne
le làcreme d'acquare.

1953

In the Fine Air

All alone
in the thin air
of my mountain
to feel within
the beat of my heart,
and outside
breathe in life
with the sigh of dawn.

Small Cloud

In the sky
the smoke from cherry bombs during a feast.
Like a veil
against the sun
it stretches, it coils;
it starts to disappear from view
fading to blue.

In the morning, a dank fog
reappears on earth
to recompose
the dewdrops
on the leaves.

La dumanna

Dalla finestra ntrava all'ampruvvise
lu matutine.
— E ddó ddó? —
Na mórra de picciune
'n ciele ze spaleiava;
argiente vive mieze a lu turchese.

Chi sa donde vulava.

Mo tutta la finestra ze spalanca
e chiù vicina,
ancora mo, resòna la dumanna.
La mórra de picciune
pare na pétta ghianca.

Ventiquattore com'a matutina.

The Question

The sound of morning bells
came suddenly through the window.
"Where? where? where?"
A band of pigeons
spread across the sky;
quicksilver over turquoise.

Where would they ever fly.

Now the whole window opens wide
and nearer,
even now, echoes the question.
The band of pigeons
looks like a white smear.

Eventide like the first hours of dawn.

Cipriesse

I

'Ncima 'n cima nu poste ze lu trova
lu potacegne
pe fa le nide a primavera.
Mentr'isse
a tutte le presenze fa nu segne,
schiùdene l'ova.

II

Fa lu guardiane
nnanze a llu cancielle.
Chieca la coccia e conta
tutte le ntrate.
Sfruscéia co lu viente
e a mezanotte
quande ze sente
areputà la cuccuvaglia,
passa la nota 'nciele.

The Cypress Tree

I

The titmouse finds a spot
right at the top
to make his nest in springtime.
While he
acknowledges all presences,
the eggs break open.

II

He stands watch
before the iron gate.
He bends his head and counts
all those who enter.
He whispers with the wind
and then at midnight
when you can hear
the owl's cry,
he passes that note on to the sky.

L'ulme

Camine e nen ze sa
da donde vé la via
né donde va.

De fore e dentre
ombre annegghiate.
Ombre arresciute
chi sa da quale storie,
da quale nonna
a tiempe de lu tiempe arracuntate.
Quill'ulme ncepponite
mo dorme allérta sule e l'aresonna.

Sapè

Sapè come ze guarda
chell'acqua pe la sete ntruvedata
pe racchiararla.

Sapé ddó corre
chell'ora de lu suonne a mezanotte
pe racchiapparla.

The Elm Tree

You walk and don't know
where the road begins
or where it leads.

From inside and out
dim shadows.
Shadows emerging
from unknown tales,
from lullabies told in the time of times.
That knotted elm tree
now sleeps standing alone and dreams them still.

To Know

To know how
you see that cloudy water through your thirst
to make it clear.

To know where
the hour of sleep is running to at midnight
to bring it back.

Lume de cunte

Z'è sfucata la vòria
mo che z'è fatta sera, e murmuréia
e porta appriesse nuvole lontane.

Na luce fa cioció
d'arrete a chi sa ddó,
e n'atra luccechéia
dentre a na massaria.
lume de cunte mieze a la memoria.

1954

Pasquarella

Dope na notte ntèra
vòta e revòta sotte a le lenzora,
dentre a nu calzettone appise
sotte a la ciminèra,
quattre fìcura secche.
Mieze a la fratta all'uorte na tagliola
senza nu passarielle.
Dentre a du uocchie nire nu surrisc.

Mo dentre a chella casa
ce sta na mamma a ride?
Ce sta nu guagliuncielle
che come allora
la mette la tagliola sott'all'uorte?
E dentre a chella stanza
chi senza suonne aspetta
la pasquarella?

1952

Fairy Tale Light

The north wind has died down
now that evening's fallen, and it murmurs
and carries in its wake faraway clouds.

A light goes peekaboo
from behind who knows where,
and another glimmers
inside a farmhouse.

Fairy-tale light within the mist of memory.

1954

The Befana

After an entire night
tossing under the bedsheets,
inside an enormous sock
hanging from the fireplace,
only four dried figs.
A trap sans sparrow
under a hedge in the kitchen garden.
A smile that gleams across two raven eyes.

Inside that house today
is there a mother's laughter?
Is there a little child
who as in those times past
still sets the bird trap
inside the kitchen garden?
And in that very room
who stays awake and waits
for the Befana?

1952

Chell'atra notte

Chesta iè come fusse n'atra notte,
— né ddó né quande fu, i' m'arecorde.
Pe líette nu saccone de scartuocce;
a quille ballecone
z'affaccia nu salustre allevedite
pe vedé se dorme.
E chiove.
Mieze a la scùrdia cóla
e conta le minute — tinghe, tinghe —
na stizza d'acqua
'ncopp'a nu cupiérche de callare.

1952

Chella luntananza

Putesse aredà luoghe
a nu spazie de tiempe
all'amore gudute,
a le pene sufferte.

Nen patì chiù d'avé pe sorta
chesta malincunia
che senz'avvise vè co l'uocchie mbusse
e a chella luntananza me straporta.

1952

That Other Night

This is as if it were another night,
— I don't remember either where or when.
For bed a mattress made of withered leaves;
An ashen flash of lightning peeks
inside that balcony
to see if I am asleep.
And it's raining.
In the darkness a drop of water trickles
and counts the minutes
— ding, ding, ding —
over the copper lid of an old cauldron.

1952

That Distance

If I could bring back
a stretch of time
the love enjoyed
the pain endured.

No longer have to bear
this melancholy
that without warning comes with moisty eyes
and carries me away to that great distance.

1952

Presepie

Tant'anne, nu minute.

Fore, la vita 'n suonne.
Le case arrampecate
strette a lu campanile
ze no sò sciute
da na curnice de presepie antiche
a lu rechiame de la campanella;
chill'ulme loche a balle
lu papazzielle a riga.
'N copp'a la neve
pedate a fila a fila.

Passa la maiellese e le scancella.

1954

Sponda

Chi z'arecorda chiù qual'è la via
che porta a chella sponda
d'acqua surgiva.
Me ce retrove come fusse 'n suonne
a resentì nu strusce de liscerta
e de nu petterusce
lu zittezitte;
a vedé scorre pe l'acqua lu ciele,
a nginocchiarme e beve a surze a surze
senza stutà la sete.

1953

Crèche

So many years, an instant.

Outside, life is a dream.
The houses clinging to the hillside
huddled against the bell tower
have emerged
from the frame of an ancient crèche
at the toll of a bell;
those elm trees down there,
figurines in a row.
On the snow
long lines of footprints.

The Maiellese passes and erases them.

1954

Springwater

Who can remember now which is the road
that leads to that small pool
of limpid spring water.
I'm standing there as if it were a dream
listening to the rustle of a lizard
and a robin's
tweet-tweet;
and watching the sky stream across the water,
down on my knees to drink in endless sips
without quenching my thirst.

1951

Maitenata

La striscia gialla de nu lampieione
a iettà neve 'n faccia a nu portone
mieze a la via e 'n cuolle a chi passava.
Senza na voce e senza chiù culore
la notte attuorne attuorne.

All'ampruvvise,
vicine e puó luntane
da ièsse a balle a loche a monte,
na sampogna arrachita
schiuppava ru taluorne,
come se stesse
a corre appriesse
chiagnenne
a quacchedune che scappava
pe mieze a chella scùrdia abbrevedita.

1952

Love Song

The yellow lightstreak coming from a streetlamp
was hurling snow in front of the large door
into the street and against passersby.
Voiceless and wholly colorless
the night was everywhere around.

Suddenly,
nearby and then farther away,
from down below to way uphill
a rasping bagpipe
broke into a wail,
as if
weeping in pursuit
of someone in swift flight
across the shivering darkness.

1952

L'uorte

Chi vè? chi vè?
Ze smove la zappetella appesa
a ru mile granare
tramenne sta sunanne ventunora:
aspetta ancora
co na pagliuca 'n mocca.

Chi vè? chi vè?
Zurréia ru canciélle arruzzenite.
Com'a na prucessione
ze sente, ma nen passa.
Na ventata z'abbassa:
nu suspire de fronne.
Pe l'aria lu respire
de le generazione.

Cascà vulanne

Fa la mbréia a nu nide;
da la ventima
piglià la voce a raccuntà nu cunte
a la mamma che cova.

Quande so scapelate le cardille,
lassà la rama
senza rumore
e mbriache d'aria
cascà vulanne.

1952

The Kitchen Garden

Who's coming? who's coming?
The hoe hanging on the pomegranate
sways lightly
with the evening tolls:
he still waits,
a straw in his mouth.

Who's coming? who's coming?
The rusty iron gate
begins to creak.
You hear something that sounds
like a procession, but it never passes.
A gust of wind drifts down:
a sigh runs through the leaves.
Across the air the breath
of generations.

To Fall Flying

To throw shade on a nest;
steal the wind's voice
to tell a story
to the mother that sits.

After the fledgling goldfinches take wing,
to leave the branch
noiselessly
and fall in flight
drunken with air.

1952

SALUSTRE

I

Le vie so tutte le méie
ca facce notte e iuorne
lu vatecare.

II

La muntagna, p'aretruvà lu spiérse
pe mieze a la chianura,
manna l'astore.

III

Éie mannate a spasse la memoria,
è festa.

IV

Dentre a la vita méia m'arencontre
e campe.

V

Sicut fur nocturnus

Quande tu rrive, quille è lu tiempe.
Nu salustre.

Lightning

I

The roads are all mine
a coachman
night and day

II

The mountain, to find
the one lost in the plain,
sends out the hawk.

III

I have sent memory out for a stroll.
It's a holiday.

IV

Within my life I find myself
and live.

V

Sicut fur nocturnus

When you arrive, that is the time.
Lightning.

Varie

Chiagne pe me?

Pecché tié l'uocchie mbusse
com'a na merìcula
che pènne da ru spéne
dope n'acqua d'aguste?
É' chiante, amore?
Chi z'ha pigliate guste
de farte chiagne, core
mié doce,
e d'appannarte l'uocchie
de làcreme e de pene?
É chiagnute pe me,
amore? E dimme,
pecché?

No pe tristizia certe
sse guance éi' sculurite,
e nvece de la risa,
ru chiante éi' misse 'nmocca;
forse pe gelusia,
ca te vuoglie sul'i';
e vularrìa
sule pe me sse sguarde,
sule pe me ssa vocca!

Perdóneme:
songhe pentite
e vuoglie nginucchiate
fa turnà co nu vasce
chiss'uocchie rischiarate.

Various

Are You Crying for Me?

Why are your eyes as moist
as a blackberry
clinging to a thorn
after an August rain?
Are they tears, my love?
Who was it that so enjoyed
making you cry,
dear heart,
and dimmed your eyes
with tears and pain?
Did you cry for me, my love?
But won't you tell me why?

Of course it isn't sadness
that turned pale on your cheeks,
and made your lips to weep
instead of laughing;
maybe it's jealousy,
because I want you to myself alone;
and I would like
that gaze for me alone,
those lips for me alone!

Forgive me:
I am truly sorry
and on my knees
I want to see a kiss
bring back the brightness in your eyes.

Esempie

Che mporta a la cannéla se ze stuta
ca l'uoglie z'è finite?
Ha fatte luce.

Che mporta a lu garòfene
se z'arechiéca 'n terra ammuscelite?
Iè state addore.

Che ce ne mporta a la mòrra de grane
se la furmica
ze la strascina?
Iè stata spica.

1951

La notte sdegnata

Vatte sfuriata e corre e fèrchia
e 'n faccia a stizza a stizza chiagne e scioscia
sdegnata,
la notte.

Ze ferma,
scianchéia, piglia l'onna e recumènza,
mpazzita de rummore.

Na stella
arrèsce e puó scumpare:
me pare
ca va facènne lume
pe recercà nu liette a lu repose.

1954

Example

What matters to the candle if it dies
because the oil is gone?
It did give light.

What matters to a carnation
if it sags to earth wilted?
It was a fragrance once.

What matters to the ear of wheat
if ants carry it away?
It was once a spike.

1951

The Raging Night

It blusters, it runs and howls
and drop by drop it weeps and lashes,
in a rage,
the night.

It stops,
it gasps, catches the wave and starts again,
insane with noise.

A star
comes out and disappears:
it seems
to cast a light
to look for any bed on which to rest.

1954

La svota

Z'affonna
com'a chiumme
pesante lu passe.
Pe copp'a la maiese sementata
la morra de curnacchie ze spaleia
e chiama e scennechéia.

Chi chiama?
dall'anne e la fatía appesantite
ru nome
sprufonna.

Z'è fatte scure e ze ntravede
la svota;
nu lume z'arrappiccia.
Ce sta, ce sta, ce sta chi me la leva
da 'n cuolle la vesazza e l'arrappénne
pe chi vé ppriésse.

Penna de piette
la pesantezza è deventata.
Nesciuna via chiù

né chiù maiése né curnacchie
sott'a ru vule.
Lu suonne antiche torna sule sule.
Viente de ciele passa, zitte zitte.

1954

The Crossroads

The footstep
sinks
like heavy lead.
Over the fallow ground already sown
a band of crows scatter and call
flapping their wings.

Whom are they calling?
Weighed down by the years and the pain
the name
drops to the depths.

It's getting dark, you can make out
the crossroads;
a light comes on again.
There is, there is, there is someone to take
the knapsack from my back and hang it up
for those who follow.

A feather from the breast
the heaviness has become.
No longer any roads
nor any fallow fields nor crows
beneath the flight.
All alone returns the ancient sleep.
A wind from the sky passes, very still.

1954

Le mazzate

Refà ru sciurarielle
'n copp'a ru muraglione.
Menà na prèta e ccide na gallina.
Sentì lluccà Nicola:
— Scappa sott'a ru ponte
ch'arriva zì Peppina. —
Refà l'abbaiareccia
appriesse a Mincantonie lu sciancate,
e può truvà pe cena le mazzate.

1950

Cipriesse

Da donda tu lu vide:
'n cima a nu colle,
'n funne a nu raserone
o mieze a nu ciardine,
siente addore de nciénze,
vide na croce e nu tavute.

Lu celeste

Sdellazza e schiuma gialle
dope l'accòta
dell'acqua ntruvedata la currente,
e a la surgente
ddó ciele addeventatte z'arrevota;
puó recumenza a corre.

Ze scopre lu celeste loche a balle.

The Spanking

To slide again
over the high wall.
To throw a stone and kill a chicken.
To hear Nicola shouting:
"Run under the bridge,
zì Peppina is coming."
To tease
Mincantonio the cripple,
and then to find a spanking set for supper.

1950

Cypress Tree

Wherever you see it:
on a hilltop,
at the end of an avenue
in the middle of a garden,
you smell the scent of incense,
you see a coffin and a cross.

The Blue

After the stream
of muddy water
the yellow current churns
and foams, and turns
toward the spring
where it became sky;
then starts to run again.

The blue appears down there over the horizon.

Mamuozie antiche

Attuorne attuorne,
tra lume e lustre
pure de mieze iuorne,
specchie pe fa paura a chi passava.

Uocchie nciufate
de mamuozie tise
dentre a lu gialle antiche.

Nnanze nu balle
de ciammaragne appise.

Da sta finestra aperta

Me guarde
a repeglià la via la matina
e puó me sperde
tra mieze a tutte quante sule sule.

Quande revè la mbréia e z'arestènne,
m'areconosche all'ùteme resuone
de la pedata
e a come vatte 'n terra lu sperdone.

Ancient Portrait

All around the room
in twilight shadow
even at high noon,
mirror to frighten those who passed before it.

A tense portrait's
troubled gaze
within the ancient yellow.

In front of it a dance
of dangling spiderwebs.

From this Open Window

I watch myself go out
early in the morning
and then get lost
alone among the people in the street.

When shadows fall again and start to spread,
I recognize myself in the last sound
of footsteps
and in the pilgrim's staff striking the ground.

Lu bielle sole

Lu bielle sole che me deva calle,
z'è fatte fridde com'a vierne vòria
che me straporta co le fronne gialle
dentr'a ru munne che nen tè memoria.

Dentr'a ru munne che nen è chiù doce
de cante e de suspire, m'arechiama;
dentr'a ru munne che nen tè chiù voce,
vatte a la porta de lu tiempe e grama.

1953

Nuvuletta

Da 'n terra iè sagliuta
e d'aria z'è ntessute
ru vele
de chella nuvuletta nnargentata,
che mentre ze ne va
pazzéia pe ru ciele.
Ze spanne, z'atturcina, z'annasconne
e ze nseréna.
A la matina 'n terra recumpare:
stizza d'acquare
'n copp'a na fronna.

The Glorious Sun

The glorious sun that used to give me warmth,
has become cold as north wind in the winter
that whisks me with the yellow leaves from earth
into a world unable to remember.

Into a world unable to rejoice
with songs and sighs, it calls me once again;
inside a world that is bereft of voice
it raps against the door of time and moans.

Little Cloud

It rose from the ground,
and the veil
of that small silver cloud,
that steals away
to play with the sky,
mingles with the air.
It stretches, it coils, it hides
and fades into the blue.
In the morning it reappears on earth:
a dewdrop
on a leaf.

Nen ce sta chiù

I

. . . na stanza, na cucina,
na finetrella pe ce fa l'amore.
Canto popolare

Ecche la luna che mo z'è llumata.
Mieze a la via vatte e va lu core;
ma quande arriva la trova abbarrata
la finestrella pe ce fa l'amore.

II

Vurrì nchianà lu ciele se putesse
co na scaluccia de sessanta passe.
Canto popolare

Ecche la scala de sessanta passe
che scegne da ru ciele fin'a 'n terra.
I' me ce appènne, ma se puó me lasse,
nen trove chiù l'amore che m'afferra.

1953

120

No Longer There

I

Look at the moon that now has grown so bright.
It spills into the street and strikes the heart;
but when it does arrive it finds it shut
the small window that kept lovers apart.

II

Look at the ladder made of sixty rungs
that from the sky descends to earth below
I cling to it, but then if I let go
I don't find love to catch me any longer.

1953

Votaciele

T'assiétte.
Nu rummore.

Nu votaciele, e passe le muntagne.
Ma nen scié tu che vule.

1951

Afa

All'uorte a balle
sott'a la fratta de sammuche
tre buche
e tre galline a rechiamaà lu galle.
Luntane
na mamma
attacca na ninna nanna.
I' miezze all'afa, e na cicala stracca.
E chiù nesciune.
A ventunora
tra titte e titte
lu strillarecce de le renenune.

1952

Dizziness

You sit down.
A noise.

Your head spins, and you cross mountains.
But it's not you that flies.

1953

Heat

Down in the kitchen garden
three holes under a bush of common elder
and three hens
calling the rooster.
Far away
a mother
begins a lullaby.
Me and a tired cicada in the heat.
And no one else.
At sunset
from rooftop to rooftop
the swallow's cry.

Lu cunte

Ce steva na vota
nu guagliuncielle
che ièttе a fa céppe,
e lu tiempe e la via
perdette.
La notte menètte
chiù scura
de la paura.
Lu guaglione sperdute
pe dentre a nu bosche
la mamma chiamava
chiamava.
Nesciune respunneva
nesciune.
'N cima a na cèrca
na checoccia vatteva lu rechiame
a lu tiempe perdute:
e tunghe e tunghe e tunghe.

Chella checoccia
steva legata
'n cima a la cèrca
e pe tutta la notte,
sbattuta da lu viente,
vatteva lu rechiame
a lu tiempe perdute:
e tunghe e tunghe e tunghe.
Na vota
la voce de lu viente respunnette:
É iute è iute è iute.

The Tale

Once upon a time
there was a child
who went out for kindling wood,
and lost
his time and bearings.
Night fell
darker
than fear.
The child lost
inside the forest
kept calling
his mother.
No one answered,
no one.
On top of an oak tree
a pumpkin marked
the beckoning to time lost:
ding ding ding.

That pumpkin
was tied
on top of the oak tree
and all night long,
lashed by the wind,
it marked the beckoning
to time lost:
ding ding ding.
Once
the voice of the wind
answered:
It's gone gone gone.

E può?
Na seggiulella cioppa,
nu guaglione assettate
nnanze a lu fuculare
ncantate a lu sentire;
na lampa che scallava
la cucina e lu scure,
n'ombra che ze moveva pe lu mure;
la voce te levava lu respire;
"Lu guaglione chiamava
chiamava;
la checoccia vatteva lu rechiame
— e tunghe e tunghe e tunghe —
tutta la notte a lu tiempe perdute."

La vòria pe la ciminèra
pur'essa arespunneva:
É iute è iute è iute.

1953

And then?
A small crippled chair,
a child seated
before the fireplace
listening enthralled;
a lamp that warmed
kitchen and darkness,
a shadow that inched along the wall;
the voice would take your breath away:
"The child called
and called;
the pumpkin marked the beckoning
— and ding ding ding —
to time lost, the whole night long."

The north wind also answered
through the fireplace:
it's gone gone gone.

1953

Presepie

Da tanta
tiempe
ogne anne — pare da sempe —
m'arresce nnanze
pe chella via
e m'areporta
a retruvà lu tiempe
de Natale
miez'all'addore de la ierva mbossa.
Sott'a ru capputtielle
le mane allevedite
porta le pupazzielle
ru muschie e la murtella.

Lu munne 'n braccia
dentr'a lu stanzone
e lu presepie
prim'accumposte 'n core
arracumponne 'n coppa a ru cascione.

Nnanze a la magnatora
stanne a guardà.
Lu Bambenielle
le vraccia
aperte
come 'n croce.

Crèche

It's been so long
now
every year — it seems for ever —
he appears before me
down that street
and brings me back
to find
that Christmas time
amid the smell of wet grass.
Ashen hands
under the overcoat,
he carries the figurines
the moss and myrtle.

The world in his arms
within the large room
and the crèche
that he'd arranged already in his heart
now he rearranges on the massive chest.

In front of the manger
they stand and watch.
The little Child
arms
open
as if upon the cross.

Cantata 'n suonne

Da dond'è partite
camina.
Puó rriva
e vatte lu core:
— tuppe tuppe tuppe.—

Entra e pe tutte le vie va nnanze.
Ze guarda attuorne ze ferma
addumanna.
La voce iè antica.

E pàssene pàssene pàssene
e nesciune te lassa,
tu rieste arrète a calata de sole
e te ze gliotte
la notte.

Negghia

Tu cale la notte
p'annasconne lu suleche
e puorte la pesantezza
l'addore e lu sudore
dell'aria.

Vierne

Scarpe sfasciate,
nfancate,
nu capputtielle,
la neve all'uorte,
nu passarielle.

Dream Song

From where he started
he walks on.
Then he arrives
and his heart pounds:
"rap rap rap."

He enters and goes through every street.
He looks around he stops
he asks.
His voice is ancient.

And they pass they pass they pass
and no one leaves you,
you're left behind with the evening shadows
and the night
swallows you.

Fog

You come down at night
to hide the furrow
and bring the heaviness
the smell and the sweat
of the air.

Winter

Muddied, broken
shoes
a small coat, snow
in the kitchen garden,
a little sparrow.

Sabate sante

La tavella faceva de campana,
nu guagliuncielle vatteva vatteva:
"tatanghe, tatanghe"
e ze scurdave
la giacchetta arrappezzate
le mane nfreddulite.
— Chi vò ì a la messa. —
— Tatanghe, tatanghe. —
Nesciune ze muveva da la casa
se quille guagliuncielle nfreddulite
nen alluccava e nen vatteva.

L'arrescallava dope
lu fuoche sante
sotte a ru campanile.

Z'alluma dentr'all'uocchie lu passate.

Picciune a morre 'n copp'a lu campanare:

stanne a cercà lu suone.

Holy Saturday

The wooden board became a bell,
a child was banging banging it:
"whack whack whack"
and would forget
his patched-up jacket
his shivering hands.
— Who wants go to mass.
"whack whack whack."
No one moved from the house
if that shivering child
did not cry or bang.

The holy fire
under the belfry
would warm him later.

The past begins to brighten in the eyes.

Bands of pigeons gathered on the belfry:

they're looking for the sound.

La nevefra

e voria e neve e neve. Arrabelate
senza sentì lu fridde.

La via lònga lònga valecava
le tre muntagne;
passava tre chianure e può tre sciume,
ntrava a nu bosche.
Nen ze vedeva lume,
ma ze sentiva 'n cupe 'n cupe
l'allucche de nu lupe.

Quaccune sbelave sbelava
la neve e me chiamava.

Dope, lu suonne.

Mamma

Lu cante
d'aria de notte a lume de la luna.

The Snowstorm

and wind and snow and snow. Buried
without feeling the cold.

The long, long road went over
the three mountains;
it crossed three plains and then three rivers,
it entered a wood.
There were no lights,
but one could hear down deep
the howling of the wolf.

Someone was digging digging
in the snow, calling me.
Afterward, sleep.

Mother

The song
of the night air against the moonlight.

Frammenti

Scegne lu suone de lu campanile
a passe a passe
a ventunora.

Arevederte com'a chella notte
attuorne la nevèfra
le ciambanielle mieze a le mustacce.

Nu passe che camina e cerca suonne

Camina
uocchie a cercà la via.
Passa matina e sera
uocchie a cercà la via
le recchie tese a resentì na voce.

La luna mo z'abbagna dent'a sciume
e z'arraggriccia.
Senza farse vedé rrete a le fratte
l'amore mo ch'è notte
nchiana la viarella.

Fragments

The sound descends from the belfry
step by step
at nightfall.

*

To see you like that night
amid the snowstorm
icicles in your moustache.

*

A footstep falls and looks for sleep

It falls
eyes seeking the way.
It passes day and night
eyes seeking the way
ears straining to hear a voice again.

*

Now the moon dips in the river
and it shivers.
Unseen behind the bushes
now that it's night
love climbs the footpath.

*

Nu liette
de fresca lupinella
pe menàrmece 'n coppa a mezanotte
e scurdarme stanchezza.

*

La luna mo z'affaccia e guard'attuorne,
splenne la faccia bella appena sponta
e manna 'n ciele tutte lu splennore.
Z'areschiara la terra,
la pace scegne 'n terra da le stelle;
trema de passione la campagna.

*

Me pare de sunnà guardanne 'n ciele.
Camine sule — e de quell'atre munne
sente lu respire,
camine sule a piede mananute
come a spartì lu grane
pe chella via polvere de stelle.

*

A la via d'annanze arevutarme
p'arracumponne e reiaprì lu core.

Arravé calle
pure se sciocca fore,
e iuorne e notte e 'n suonne . . .

138

*

A bed
of fresh sainfoin
on which to lie at midnight
and forget weariness.

*

Now the moon peeps out and looks around,
her lovely face glows radiant as it looms
and casts her splendor throughout the whole sky.
The earth grows bright,
peace descends from the stars upon the earth;
and the countryside is quivering with passion.

*

I seem to be in a dream watching the sky.
I walk alone — and I feel the breath
from that other world,
I walk alone and barefoot
as if to part the wheat
stardust through that path.

*

To turn and look before me
so I can compose and open my heart again.

To feel warm again
even if it snows outside,
and day and night and in my dreams . . .

*

Mo tutta la finestra
ze spalanca,
chiù cupe è lu turchese de lu ciele.
Lu vule de picciune
chiù luntane.

*

Smove l'ombra ru viente
e cerca pace.

*

Ru munne z'areschiara e tu returne.
La viarella stretta ze sturceva.
Na rosa appena schiusa messa mpiette
la bellezza che 'n faccia te rideva.

*

Dent'a lu tiempe e l'ora
lu sole z'è fermate
senza cumande.
E tu returne
com'a na rosa appena schiusa.

*

Now the whole window
opens wide,
the turquoise of the sky is growing deeper.
A flight of pigeons
in the distance.

*

The wind nudges the shadow
and seeks peace.

*

The world is growing bright and you return.
The narrow footpath swerved.
Pinned to your breast a rose just now unfolded
beauty that smiled upon your face.

*

Within time and hour
the sun has stopped
unbidden.
And you come back
like a rose just now unfolding.

Afterword

Eugenio Cirese's poetic itinerary subsumes all the seasons of Molisan poetry in dialect. From the 1920s on, there is no stage or period in which Cirese's presence has not seemed determining and influential. For a trenchant and persuasive rereading of his poetic works, it is therefore necessary to follow the iter of his varied and complex poetic development in its relationship with the cultural and social milieu of the Molisan province and, in particular, to retrace his first poetic phase, deliberately downplayed by the author himself. In reality, his commitment to the attainment of an essential poetry, in keeping with the most important and decisive achievements of both dialect and Italian poetry within the framework of twentieth-century poetics, led him to make choices and rejections in his work, at times excessively harsh. But if this bears witness to the absolute rigor of his research, it can be misleading for an objective diachronic analysis, which must concern not only the four collections that earmark Cirese's poetic season — *Suspire e risatelle* (Sighs and Snickers, 1918), *Rugiade* (Dew, 1932), *Lucecabelle* (Fireflies, 1951) and, published posthumously, *Poesie molisane* (Molisan Poems, 1955) — but also the chapbooks that preceded the first and second books and for the most part were not included in them, the collections of folksongs and the dialect prose.

Eugenio Cirese's poetry is rooted in the late-Romantic culture of the latter part of the nineteenth century, in which the original predilection for the folksong combined with erudite research of popular traditions and with a reassessment of dialect, and in the emotional inclination to interpret fixed, restless or recurring attitudes of the Molisan people's soul. It is not by chance that the first significant, if scanty, compilation, *Canti popolari e sonetti in dialetto molisano* (Folksongs and Sonnets in the Molisan Dialect, 1910), contains songs "gathered among the people" and transcribed "in their rustic but expressive simplicity" with the addition of a few sonnets written "during the lulls of the mind." They are both the expression of the Molisan dialect which has, "maybe more than so many others in Italy, spontaneity of expression and strength of feeling." The sonnets counterbalanced the musical cadence of the folksongs with realistic impressions of everyday life; like those which, two years later in another pamphlet, *La Guerra (discursi di cafuni)* (The War [Peasants' Conversations]), recorded the moods of the farmers during the Libyan War, alternating between surges of nationalistic pride, grief for the fallen and a mother's heartrending tears for her faraway wounded son.

Cirese's early poetic work is based essentially on the conviction that there is an inseparable link between folksongs and dialect poetry: a conviction that will remain constant and unaltered with time, and which inspired an unforgettable autobiographical page in the premise to *Canti popolari del Molise* (Folksongs from Molise) (1953) forty years later:

> I was born when the studies of folk poetry had been flourishing for a while, often with an undisciplined exuberance. Urbanization was yet to become a worrisome phenomenon, and emigration was just beginning. The latter, if it took hands away from the fields, it filled the mailboxes with lire at a very favorable exchange and permitted a fundamental revolution in the history of the *Mezzogiorno*: the transfer of small and medium-sized properties from the *galantuomo* to the farmer who acquired it with the savings of years of work, heavy and disheartening, on the other side of the ocean.

But the phenomenon still did not disturb the dreams of the carefree middle class at the close of the century, and in the towns they still sang a lot; they also drank and made love. I began at that time to collect songs, to learn them and to sing them. I later compiled them and found my own voice in the language of the people.

Cirese'a early work is contained in *Suspire e risatelle* (1918). The title itself, deliberately subdued, is indicative of Cirese's initial twofold inspiration — the musical abandon of the love songs and the keen observation of the attitudes of townspeople and farmers with respect to ordinary and extraordinary events (Libyan war, the war of 1915-8). Moreover, the "realistic" bent is not to be taken as a subjective and, in a manner of speaking, ideological involvement: it has been poignantly observed that Cirese knew how to generate a vein of humor through the contact between the mindset of the people and more refined, cultured thought. As for the poetic achievements, those more convincing and authentic seem to be the "passionate songs," in which the love elegy is not always able to strike a firm balance of tone, but the already refined and skillful echoing of popular "airs" foreshadows the best Cirese.

After the 1920s, following the end of the phase we could define as being both philological and late-Romantic, Cirese's cultural development — also considering his direct and active involvement in the everyday reality of the Molisan school — takes place under the aegis of Giovanni Gentile's cultural and educational policies. *Gente buona* (Good People) — a primer for the schools of Molise — published in 1925 by Carabba in Lanciano, carries in the title page an explicit reference to the programs of 1923 and the official approval of the Ministry of Public Education. Compiled with unquestionable didactic skill, being the product of a personal and at the same time collective experience in the schools of Molise, adapted to the academic calendar and the georgic changing of seasons and months, the book is an orderly and balanced anthology of passages on geography, history, regional art and culture, notions of agriculture relating to seasonal products, news about fair and markets, advices about hygiene, prose and poetry in dialect where, next to Cirese, appear the names of Altobello and Sassi. The result is a realistic picture of social and economic life, largely conditioned by agricultural production, and marginally by handicrafts: a truthful image of the Molise of the 1920s (and of other decades as well), and of a large part of the *Mezzogiorno*; and an expression of a gratifying idea of rural life and the traditional values it implied. And if something new, like the construction of a hydroelectric plant, appears in the life of the province, Cirese records it ("La 'lettricità" [Electricity], 1926) in the bafflement of the Molisan farmer who tackles the problems and terminology of scientific innovation.

In 1932, to conclude the second phase of his work, Cirese published his second compendium of poems, *Rugiade*. In it, the tones of Cirese's poetry range from the musical motifs of folksongs to realistic impressions of everyday life, from signed "tunes" to legends lost in time (*Ru cantone de la fata* [The Fairy's Rock]), and sung again in the metrical and narrative pattern of the octave. With respect to *Suspire e risatelle*, the essential novelty of *Rugiade* is the rejection of most of the "passionate songs," which in the first *corpus* expressed the extreme tension of melodic abandon, replaced by didactic, fable-centered, gnomic poems, on the whole "ideological." The verses placed as premise to this last section of the collection (Don't be conceited: / read and think, / because even a peasant / can teach you something) represent its explicit interpretive key, in absolute consonance with Lombardo Radice's speech to the teachers of Florence. The "culture" of the "illiterate" people, rediscovered by the teacher, can accept and assimilate in its unchanging mindset even the novelties brought by time.

The overall sense of Cirese's cultural position in those years is clearly defined in the premise to *Rugiade*, where the vindication of the contribution of his research on

145

folksongs and dialect poetry to the reconstruction of the cultural, and consequently geographical and historical, identity of Molise, is inserted on purpose in the political and cultural context of the time (also to be remembered is his attempt at dialect prose — *Tempo d'allora: figure, storie e proverbi* [Time of long ago: figures, tales and proverbs] (1939) — in the tradition of the regional sketch):

> The true and profound origin of the spirit and character of a region is its dialect, as the origin of the unity of conscience of a nation is its language.
>
> To deny the unity of language means to deny the Nation, to deny the unity of dialect means to deny the Region, to deprive dialect art of its content and its essential function, which is to celebrate the region with the heart and language of everyone, to advance, with everyone, toward the possession of new values. Because the spirit of the people evolves, is nourished, ascends: it elevates its forms, it widens the horizons of its life. The thought of a region that forty years ago had ninety per cent illiteracy is not the thought of the region that shame has reduced today to five per cent. A people that from the cult of God and family has risen with one leap to the virginal concept and the cult of the Fatherland and accepts with joy the present in which it believes, lives and hopes, now loves its history with a different heart already, it raises with a different voice the hymn to its labor, it looks with different eyes at its mountains. And beyond the mountains.
>
> There are, however, still some who confuse dress and body, form and content, and conclude that in a region there are as many dialects and sub-dialects as there are townships.

I am waiting for them to recognize their error. And they will have to recognize it because the National Government has given the Region back its face and its unitary function; because — and it's due to Giovanni Gentile — dialect has been given an educational purpose in the school, and because dialect poetry no longer has digestive duties at suppers and town banquets: it does not cackle and scratch about along the unpaved roads of the villages any more: it has put on voice and feathers and has discovered the joy of song and flight.

Such explicit statements leave no doubts as to Cirese's adherence to the political-cultural orientation of the period which today is referred to as "the years of consent" to Fascism (in the premise cited there is also a winking allusion to *Strapaese*), and explain, therefore, his "belatedness," noted by Pasolini, with respect to twentieth-century poetics.

Cirese's third book of poetry, *Lucecabelle*, (Rome, 1951) was published about twenty years after *Rugiade*, with the author's remark that the poems of the first group belong to the years 1913-1932, and that the subsequent ones, unpublished, were composed after 1944. Even in an unquestionably new collection, Cirese does not forego giving the reader a compendium of his previous work: but this time, choosing the songs that had also been set to music ("Canzunetta," "Torna l'amore" and "Canzone d'atre tiempe"), and above all some of the "passionate songs" of *Suspire e risatelle* that had not been included in *Rugiade*, the selection appears rigorous and essential because it obeys a uniform criterion, which is certainly not anthological. With the elimination of the realistic verse, the more traditionally musical poems are recovered by virtue of a new reading, more mindful of the neo-Romantic tones and the formal values that it expressed and heralded *in nuce*. To give sense and depth to this renewal in continuity of inspiration, there is the second group of poems, *La fatìa* (Work). The traditional

147

realistic element — the interminable toil of the Molisan farmer, summer and winter, with the sun or in a storm, "sky to see and ground to tread on" — is assumed and transcended in a desolate metaphor of the human condition.

Severed from his human roots, existentially defeated in life's long journey toward death, bound only by a slender thread to the Christian acceptance of destiny (evident are the signs of the war turmoil impressed in Cirese's heart), the poet seems to draw only from the airy, serene vastness of the sky the freedom and redemption from earthly ruins: a few poems — "Lucecabelle," "Vulà", "L'astore" — express this ethical and emotional tension in a phonic and verbal lightness of absolute purity. Even the memories of the past, his childhood in particular, come back sharp but almost immaterial, in a light of memory devoid of any elegiac or pathetic redundance, as moments of an unappeased search for the "innocent land." Here, almost textually, some of the motifs of the early Cirese reappear, like the the insistent return of the lullaby:

Sleep, my beauty, sleep peacefully
a sleep that lasts the whole night long

and of

Let me, guitar, let me be a child again
let me be innocent

already found in *Suspire e risatelle*. But now devoid of the emotional urgency and episodic inspiration, they acquire a tone "decidedly evocative in the best literary sense" (F. Ulivi), and become sounds and signs of a disenchanted readiness for death. *Lucecabelle* represents the highest moment in Cirese's poetry. But the same unity of tone and style distinguishes the *Nuove poesie* (New Poems) — which the poet had already approved for publication just before his

148

death, and which came out posthumously in *Poesie Molisane*, edited by F. Ulivi and A.M. Cirese, 1955. With the exception of "Lu muortecille" (The Dead Child), a long elegy of childhood felled *ante diem*, the fragments of memory, interruptions and pauses of the silence of time, are fixed in the expressive terseness of lines like: "Lume de cunte mieze a la memoria," or in compressed melodies, like "Spazeià" (To Range), one of Cirese's most beautiful poems, metrically flawless (the rhythm of the endecasyllables first interrupted by the pause of the seven-syllable line, and starting again with a vertical progression that the last line stresses and highlights), which conveys the sudden start, the intermittence of the heart before the lunar enchantment. The expressive tension achieves extreme effects of epigraphic conciseness in the last poems. *Salustre* (Lightning), are the flashes that illuminate, in the silence of time, the few, stark signs of a life accepted without illusions:

> Within life I find myself
> and live.

until the moment that reveals death:

> When you arrive, that is the time.
> Lightning.

A diachronic look at Cirese's poetic career has allowed us to distinguish, in the continuity of a long, tormented work of linguistic and stylistic refinement, with rejections and afterthoughts, two seasons with different poetic properties corresponding to different and distant cultural climates.

In the first period, from the beginning until *Rugiade*, more than the divergence between musicality and realism (which alternate with differentiations which are only thematic), there is the nearly exclusive intent to provide an objective an pictorial image of the world of the Molisan peo-

149

ple; image and representation which involve the poet's emotional participation in a deliberately reductive conception of his own indispensable cultural mediation. It cannot be suggested that such an orientation be perceived as a presumed contradiction "between a socialistic objectivation and a religious introversion" (P.P. Pasolini). In reality, in the poetics of the early Cirese, it is not possible to detect any basis for this type of intentions and attitudes, because the "objective" representation of the popular world implied the consonance of straightforward and essential religiousness as a comfort to hope and life, just as reclaiming the rural "myth" and the regional specificity revealed integration and consent with the most conspicuous aspects and themes of the years of Fascism.

Cirese's transition to a new poetic season is marked by the existential experience during the years of the Second World War, by the poet's physical separation from his region, by the general recovery after the war, with its intense, fervent intermingling of cultural orientations and perspectives, and by a longing for deprovincialization. Cirese furnished a few concise but lucid and convincing insights into the radical renewal of his poetry in reply to questions posed by P.P. Pasolini:

> Dialect is a language. In order for it to be a means of poetic expression and transform itself into literary language and images, it is necessary that it be possessed totally; that one be conscious of its cultural content and its human expressive power. In my childhood and early youth . . . I have spoken, I have collected songs, I have been happy, I have wept, *thought* in dialect.

> I am not about to maintain the greater expressive effectiveness of dialect over the literary language — a commonplace without merit, because every language has fullness and effectiveness of forms: I am only say-

150

ing that the possession of dialect facilitates the search for forms in effective attitudes and proper imagery: in sum, it increases the possibility of giving — and this is for me the vital need of dialect poetry — something new to itself and, why not?, to the literary language (1953).

Cirese will make the poetic significance of *Lucecabelle* (1951) explicit: no longer the use of dialect in the sense of memory and vernacular reconstruction, thus rooted in an "objective" or realistic *mimesis*, but rather chosen exclusively to serve a subjective expressive need, for a linguistic incisiveness and stylistic poignancy more appropriate and suitable to literary language. Thus, it is not by chance that calques and transpositions from Italian to dialect, present to a conspicuous degree in so much "poetry in dialect" of the twentieth century, are not detectable in Cirese's poetry.

Cirese's approach to the formal methods characteristic of twentieth-century poetic experiences may seem different, but only *prima facie*. As was said already, Cirese's poetic work, through selections, rejections and linguistic probings, was inspired by a rigorous tension toward a rarefied expressiveness at the edge of silence, which was in harmony with twentieth-century sensibility and its quest for an "essential" poetry. Reduced to its mythic, original purity, the Molisan dialect — which had no literary precedents and was almost totally entrusted to oral tradition — became part, with the timbre of Eugenio Cirese's poetic voice, of the literary history of the Italian twentieth century.

Luigi Biscardi

AGMV Marquis

MEMBER OF THE SCABRINI GROUP
Quebec, Canada
2000